CHELTEN IN 50 BUILDINGS

DAVID ELDER

AMBERLEY

To Winifred

First published 2017

Amberley Publishing, The Hill, Stroud
Gloucestershire GL5 4EP

www.amberley-books.com

British Library Cataloguing in Publication Data.
A catalogue record for this book is available from the British Library.

ISBN 978 1 4456 7320 2 (print)
ISBN 978 1 4456 7321 9 (ebook)

Origination by Amberley Publishing.
Printed in Great Britain.

Contents

Key

Introduction

In 1944 an influential report on Cheltenham by the Georgian Group observed that a town is 'a composite work of art, good or bad, to the making of which many generations of men have made their contribution' and that 'a few towns have had the good fortune to be built with unity of purpose and at a time when contemporary taste was at a high level'. It went on to identify Cheltenham as possessing 'the rare quality of "urbanity" – of good manners – raised sometimes to such a standard of excellence that the town becomes architecturally speaking a national possession and its residents the holders of a great responsibility'. In this selection of some of Cheltenham's most iconic buildings I have attempted to meet this 'great responsibility' by presenting a rounded, balanced view of the town's architectural gems. I focus not merely on its well-known Regency heritage but also celebrate the rare surviving examples from its medieval and Georgian past, as well as highlighting some less well-known examples to illustrate how the town has embraced styles as diverse as Italian Renaissance, Gothic Revival, Arts and Crafts, Edwardian baroque, and art deco. Cheltenham has never been 'stuck in the past' and its recent legacy also includes some bold examples of modern architecture, including the controversial Eagle Tower built in the 1960s, GCHQ's unmissable twenty-first-century 'Doughnut', and the £45-million redevelopment at Prestbury Park, the home of National Hunt racing.

Although Iron Age forts existed on both Leckhampton and Cleeve hills and a Neolithic long barrow (*c.* 4000–2000 BC) was reputedly excavated in the town in 1832, the first recorded mention of Cheltenham was in AD 803 when it was known as Celtan hom, possibly deriving from 'well-watered valley [hamm] of (the hill called) Cilta or Celta'. By the sixteenth century Cheltenham had developed along one long thoroughfare, the antiquarian John Leland referring to it as Cheltenham Street and describing it as 'a longe toune havynge a market'. From 1716 Cheltenham gradually developed as a spa resort after mineral wells were discovered on farmland, reputedly from 'pidgeons pecking at the calcareous particles for the digestion of their food'. The turning point in the town's fortunes came in 1788 following a five-week visit by George III. The town's new-found popularity continued its momentum after 1800, its population increasing fourfold between 1801 and 1821. By the middle of the nineteenth century its importance can be gauged from the fact that, in 1854, it could boast the installation of pillar letter boxes eight months before London.

However, the fashion of spa water drinking declined steadily from the 1830s onwards, and by the 1850s a gradual shift was taking place from pleasure-seeking at the spa towards evangelical preaching and learning as Cheltenham reinvented itself as a centre for religion and education. Today, the town's wealth of churches, chapels and colleges bears witness to this. Later, the town also developed itself as a centre for sport, particularly horse racing, festivals, shopping and the service sector.

The 50 Buildings

St Mary's Church, renamed Cheltenham Minster in 2013, is by far the oldest building in the town, the arches under its tower dating back to around 1170. It is believed that this Grade I-listed building replaced a Saxon church, probably erected four centuries earlier. At the time of the Domesday Book in 1086 the church belonged to Reinbald, Edward the Confessor's chancellor. Later, in 1131 Henry I granted it to Cirencester Abbey, following which the Augustinian canons built the present church. It then remained in the abbey's ownership until the Dissolution of the Monasteries in 1539. The church was then leased to a succession of laymen, including notably the philosopher and statesman Francis Bacon.

Originally, the laymen were responsible for appointing curates to serve the church and parish, but this right later transferred to Jesus College, Oxford, then to Joseph Pitt, the developer of Pittville, and subsequently to Revd Charles Simeon, the evangelical clergyman who appointed Revd Francis Close, Cheltenham's most famous and controversial rector. Close remained as the perpetual curate of the church for thirty years, founding and supporting several churches and educational institutions in the town before moving to become Dean of Carlisle in 1856.

Among the church's many notable features is some fine nineteenth-century stained glass. Of the many memorials, one of particular interest is dedicated to Henry Skillicorne,

Cheltenham's oldest building.

Above: The rose window with fourteenth-century tracery and Victorian glass.

Right: Henry Skillicorne's memorial, reputedly the longest in the country.

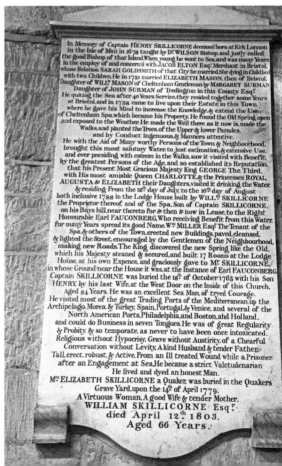

In Memory of Captain HENRY SKILLICORNE deceased born at Kirk Lonnon in the Isle of Man in 1678 taught by Dr WILSON Bishop, and justly called the good Bishop of that Island,When young he went to Sea,and was many Years in the employ of and concern'd with JACOB ELTON Esqr Merchant in Bristol, whose Relation SARAH GOLDSMITH of that City he married,She dying in Childbed with two Children,He in 1731 married ELIZABETH MASON, then of Bristol. Daughter of WILL^m MASON of Cheltenham Gentleman by MARGARET SURMAN Daughter of JOHN SURMAN of Tredington in this County Esqr He quiting the Sea after 40 Years Service,they resided together some Years at Bristol,and in 1738 came to live upon their Estate in this Town. where he gave his Mind to increase the Knowledge,& extend the Use of Cheltenham Spa,which became his Property, He found the Old Spring open and exposed to the Weather He made the Well there as it now is,made the Walks,and planted the Trees,of the Upper & lower Parades,
and by Conduct ingenuous,& Manners attentive,
He with the Aid of Many worthy Persons of the Town & Neighbourhood, brought this most salutary Water to just estimation,& extensive Use. and ever presiding with esteem in the Walks, saw it visited with Benefit, by the greatest Persons of the Age, and so established its Reputation, that his Present Most Gracious Majesty King GEORGE The Third, with His most amiable Queen CHARLOTTE,& the Princesses ROYAL AUGUSTA & ELIZABETH their Daughters,visited it drinking the Water, & residing From the 12th day of July, to the 16th day of August both inclusive 1788 in the Lodge House built by WILL^m SKILLICORNE the Proprietor thereof, and of the Spa, Son of Captain SKILLICORNE, on his Bays hill,near thereto for & then & now in Lease, to the Right Honourable Earl FAUCONBERG,Who receiving Benefit from this Water, for many Years spread its good Name. Wm MILLER Esqr The Tenant of the Spa,& others of the Town,erected new Buildings,paved,cleansed, & lighted the Street, encouraged by the Gentlemen of the Neighbourhood, making new Roads.The King discovered the new Spring like the Old. which his Majesty steaned & secured,and built 17 Rooms at the Lodge House, at his own Expence, and graciously gave to Mr SKILLICORNE, in whose Ground near the House it was,at the Instance of Earl FAUCONBERG. Captain SKILLICORNE was buried the 18th of October 1763 with his Son HENRY, by his last Wife,at the West Door on the Inside of this Church. Aged 84 Years. He was an excellent Sea Man, of tryed Courage. He visited most of the great Trading Ports of the Mediterranean,up the Archipelago, Morea & Turkey, Spain, Portugal,& Venice, and several of the North American Ports,Philadelphia,and Boston, and Holland. and could do Business in seven Tongues. He was of great Regularity & Probity, & so temperate, as never to have been once intoxicated. Religious without Hypocrisy, Grave without Austirity, of a Chearful Conversation without Levity, A kind Husband & tender Father. Tall, erect, robust, & Active, From an Ill treated Wound while a Prisoner after an Engagement at Sea,He became a strict Valetudenarian
He lived and dyed an honest Man.
Mrs ELIZABETH SKILLICORNE a Quaker, was buried in the Quakers Grave Yard,upon the 14th of April 1779.
A Virtuous Woman, A good Wife & tender Mother.
WILLIAM SKILLICORNE Esqr
died April 12th 1803.
Aged 66 Years.

a Manx sea captain who developed Cheltenham's first spa. Reputed to be the longest memorial in the country, it provides a summary of his life and achievements, the final section providing insight into his character: 'He was of great Regularity & Probity, & so temperate as never to have been once intoxicated. Religious without Hypocrisy, Grave without Austerity, of a Cheerful Conversation without Levity, A kind Husband and tender Father.' Other memorials reflect Cheltenham's close Anglo-Indian connections during the nineteenth century, while outside on the southern side of the churchyard path, there are three brass measuring marks, which were once used for measuring rope and cloth when the churchyard was used for the town's market.

2. Leckhampton Court, Church Road

Leckhampton Court, today a Sue Ryder Care hospice providing residential and day-care support for cancer patients, is the oldest surviving medieval house in Cheltenham. It has a rich and varied history with parts of the current building dating from around 1330, when it was built by Sir John Giffard whose effigy lies in nearby St Peter's Church. In fact, the

Aerial view of the court.

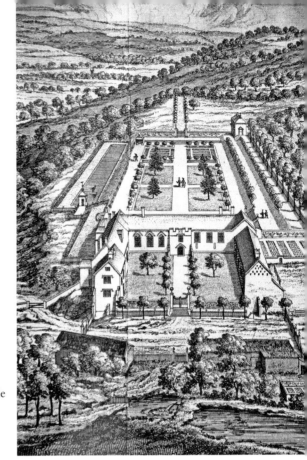

Right: The court's present layout is recognisable from Johannes Kip's 1712 engraving (detail).

Below: Doorway in the domestic area of the hall block built in 1582.

history extends back even further to Saxon times, when Leckhampton formed part of the royal manor of Cheltenham, although from at least 1066 it evidently had increasingly independent status.

In medieval times, the manor belonged to the Giffard family until 1486, when it passed by marriage to another prominent family, the Norwoods, who remained lords of the manor for approximately 300 years and whose name is still recognised through local street names and the Norwood Arms pub. It was the Norwoods who built most of the current structure, including the exquisite half-timbered Tudor wing, and planned the present layout of the house on three sides of a courtyard. At the end of the eighteenth century the manor passed once again through marriage, this time to the Trye family. One of their most distinguished family members was Charles Brandon Trye, the first to recognise the potential for serious commercial exploitation of the quarries on Leckhampton Hill, thereby providing the builders of Regency Cheltenham with a ready supply of stone.

Despite this, the Tryes experienced financial problems that necessitated the sale of the estate to John Hargreaves, a socialite and reputed friend of the Prince of Wales (later Edward VII). Between 1915 and 1919, the house served as a Red Cross hospital, during which approximately 1,700 British, Commonwealth and Belgian soldiers were cared for by Gloucestershire Voluntary Aid Detachment (VAD) staff. Then, during the Second World War the house and its surroundings accommodated American servicemen stationed there prior to the D-Day landings, and also, between 1945 and 1948, approximately 500 German prisoners of war. Thereafter it became a preparatory boarding school for a short time before falling into state of disrepair until it was rescued from demolition by Sue Ryder in 1976.

3. Charlton Park, Cirencester Road

When the diarist John Byng travelled on horseback extensively throughout England and Wales between 1781 and 1794, one of the places he visited was Cheltenham. 'In the evening', he wrote in *The Torrington Diaries*, 'I rode out and was soon driven back by the rain, but not before I had gone thro' some pleasant lanes, and cross'd several pastoral streams in the village of Charlton, 1 mile distant; near which is a neat house, belonging to Mr Prin, with a small deer park, and in a dry clean soil, which is a rarity abt Cheltenham.' The house mentioned by Byng, now part of St Edward's School, was built in 1701. It encased an earlier

The south front
of Charlton Park.

Right: The hall (now chapel) where George III was probably welcomed.

Below: The Chinese Chippendale staircase with barricade to meet school safety standards.

timber-framed house called Forden House (renamed Charlton Park from around 1784) that was constructed around 1562–68. In fact, this house was predated by an earlier hunting lodge dating from 1041, which belonged to Edward the Confessor before the estate's ownership passed to William the Conqueror at the time of the Domesday Book in 1086.

Today, the present building still retains many remarkable features. Its cellar, for example, which recently served as the school's photographic darkroom, is the oldest part and dates from the medieval period. A magnificent Chinese Chippendale staircase, installed during refurbishment work in the eighteenth century, also survives, and may have been in place by 1788 when George III was entertained here during his visit to Cheltenham. A bird's-eye view of the house and the grounds can be seen in a painting of 1748 by Thomas Robins in The Wilson art gallery and museum.

More recently, the sisters of La Sainte Union acquired the house in 1939 and converted it into a Roman Catholic school for girls. From 1987 it then became St Edward's senior school.

4. Sandford Mill, Sandford Mill Road

Although the present building, today a private house, only dates back to 1780, a corn mill operated on this site from medieval times when it belonged to Cirencester Abbey until the end of the nineteenth century. In Cheltenham's entry for the Domesday Book (1086) the mill was recorded as being either one of two 'rendering 11s.3d.' or one of three additional mills that in 1066 had helped to supply the royal dogs with 3,000 loaves annually. The choice of site for the building was originally dictated by a waterfall along the River Chelt created by water cascading over hard bands of limestone. Among the mill owners were the Cox family, who gave their name to the neighbouring field known as Cox's Meadow. By 1929 the mill machinery had been sold and the mill converted into a farm. It became derelict from the 1950s before it was restored and converted to domestic use during the 1980s.

A corn mill has operated on this site since medieval times.

Lithograph drawn by Henry Lamb, *c.* 1824–25.

5. Royal Crescent

One of Cheltenham's finest architectural treasures, with very fine ornamental ironwork, is this impressive concave crescent of Regency houses. Built on the former Church Meadow, it was constructed in stages from 1805 to the early 1820s as fashionable lodgings for visitors to the spa. Corresponding closely with equivalent crescents in other spas such as Bath and Leamington, it set the architectural style for the developing town. It now ranks as Cheltenham's oldest surviving Regency building. Following the purchase of the land from the Earl of Essex, it was Joseph Pitt's first building project in the town. It was designed by the Bath architect Charles Harcourt Masters, who also built Bath's Sydney Gardens at the end of the eighteenth century. Originally conceived as two blocks of twelve houses divided by a roadway, the structure was later adjusted to form a single crescent of eighteen houses. In 1806 No. 6 was put on the market as a fully furnished house comprising a drawing room, a breakfast parlour and nine bedrooms.

Famous inhabitants include the Duke of Gloucester, who lived at No. 18, the end house, where in 1830 he entertained Princess Victoria on her only visit to Cheltenham, and Dr Henry Charles Boisragon, physician extraordinary to George IV, who treated Lord Byron in 1812 while practising at No. 11. Today, the Royal Crescent includes some office accommodation and, since 1949, has lost some of its grandeur following the decision to enlarge the town's bus station into its front garden! Commenting on this, the poet Lady Margaret Sackville once said, 'To replace the miniature park of Royal-crescent by a bus park is to exchange a living poem for hard prose.' On the positive side, however, the crescent still retains some of the best examples of wrought ironwork in the town, including the original brackets once used to hold oil lamps above the front door.

Above: Originally built as fashionable lodgings for visitors to the spa.

Below left: Oil lamp bracket, one example of the ornamental ironwork.

Below right: Interior view showing coving and over door fanlight.

6. Cheltenham Playhouse, Bath Road

The building that since 1945 has housed the Playhouse community theatre was originally erected as a set of baths, then known as Montpellier Baths. Constructed between 1806 and 1809 for the Liverpool and London banker Henry Thompson, who also developed the Montpellier Spa, it is one of the town's unique buildings. Drawing water from nearby wells, the facilities initially offered a range of warm, cold, vapour and sulphur baths, the warm saline baths being advertised as particularly good for 'scrofulous afflictions'. However, Thompson also recognised early on the commercial advantages of adding a salts manufactory to the site so that crystallised salts could be produced through the evaporation of mineral water and then sold elsewhere. This allowed customers to benefit from their health-giving properties without having to visit the town. Perhaps the bath's most famous

Originally constructed as baths, the building has housed the Playhouse theatre since 1945.

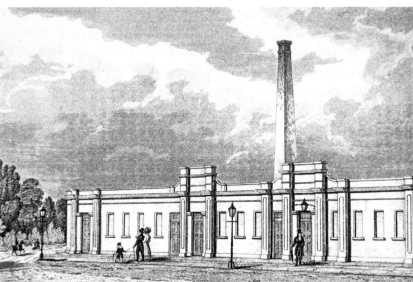

The original baths with salts manufactory.

One of the large decorative stained-glass windows.

visitor in its early years was Arthur Wellesley, 1st Duke of Wellington, who came here in 1828, where he read the daily newspapers held on a frame while lounging in a warm bath.

Despite the early success, a disastrous flood from the nearby River Chelt in 1855 provided a significant setback, so much so that, despite various improvements, it became necessary to sell the baths to Cheltenham Borough Council in 1899. A year later it reopened offering medical treatments and a public swimming pool. Large decorative stained-glass windows were also installed. However, it struggled to make a profit and by 1939 faced possible dereliction. Nevertheless, on 9 April 1945 it received a new lease of life when it opened as a community theatre, then known as the Civic Playhouse, reputedly the only new theatre to begin operating during the Second World War. Today, the theatre is run as a charity and has recently celebrated its seventieth anniversary. However, many spectators remain oblivious to the fact that the auditorium is built above a former swimming pool, the stage being positioned directly above the deep end.

7. Martin & Co., No. 19 Promenade

One of the surviving buildings from Cheltenham's early development at the north end of the Promenade has been occupied by Martin & Co., the jewellers, since 1841. Previously, it formed part of a set of Regency shops that were known as the Colonnade, the original vision being to create the 'finest line of buildings that Europe can boast' with sixty-four elegant houses, including a covered promenade leading to the well. In the end, however, only six were built and all of these, with this one exception, were demolished in the 1930s. Although some of the Colonnade buildings dated from 1791, Martin & Co.'s building was

Above: The sole surviving shop from the Colonnade buildings.

Below: Mosaic at the shop's entrance.

The Cheltenham Gold Cup handcrafted by Martin & Co. every year.

constructed after 1809 since that was when Samuel Harward, the original developer, died, instructing his wife in his will to complete its construction and furnish it as a boarding house.

However, it is not just the building that is an integral part of the town. The firm itself has enjoyed a close and enduring association with Cheltenham that surpasses 210 years. Prior to its move to the Colonnade, the clockmaker and founder of the firm Samuel Martin ran his business at No. 401 High Street from as early as 1806. By the time George Rowe published his famous *Illustrated Cheltenham Guide* in 1845 the company included an additional partner, becoming known as Messrs. Martin, Baskett, and Martin, and advertised itself as jewellers and watchmakers to the queen. Their stock was said to comprise 'every novelty in superb Plate, brilliant Gems, magnificent Jewellery, English and Foreign clocks and watches, and elegant and useful articles of Electro Plate' and its shop frontage was described as being of 'chaste and elegant design'. In 1890, George Dimmer, the mayor of Cheltenham and founder member of the Rotary Club of Cheltenham, acquired the business, changing its name to Martin & Co., and the following year Queen Victoria presented the company with a formal royal warrant. By 1912 Martin & Co. became one of the first limited companies in the country, and in 1935 the company was given the privilege of creating the Cheltenham Gold Cup for the National Hunt Racing festival, and this tradition has continued ever since.

8. Normandy House, Nos 305–309 High Street

One of the Grade II-listed buildings that most reflects Cheltenham's interesting and varied past is Normandy House. Originally known as Segrave House, it was built as a private residence in 1813 on land that was leased from Corpus Christi College, Oxford. Through the Segrave name it was closely associated with the prestigious Berkeley family who dominated much of the town's social and political life at the beginning of the nineteenth century. Colonel William Fitzhardinge Berkeley, who was the family's leading member and a strong supporter of the Cheltenham Races, became Baron Segrave in 1831. However, eight years later, after a tower extension was added, the house was converted into the town's first general hospital and dispensary. A wing was then added to accommodate two wards, each containing twenty beds, and an operating theatre. In 1845 there were six physicians,

The front façade of
Normandy House.

Segrave House when
it served as the town's
first hospital.

four surgeons and a resident house surgeon catering for an annual turnover of 5,000 outpatients and 300 inpatients. However, its use as a hospital was short-lived since, by 1849, a new hospital had been built in Sandford Road, although the building was still used to treat invalided officers returning from the Crimean War (1853–56).

In 1850 the wards of the hospital served as dormitories for the lady students of St Mary's Hall, the town's residential teacher training college, before the new St Mary's Hall (today part of the University of Gloucestershire) was built. In 1869 it was renamed Idmiston House and, later, from the 1930s housed the insurance company General Accident, and then, subsequently, local tax and social security offices. For a while, the top floor of the building was also used as a dance hall. More recently, after a period of dereliction it was restored in 1992 and became the headquarters of a specialist French tour operator, hence its current name, Normandy House. Today, its tenants comprise a wide variety of small businesses.

9. The Rotunda, Montpellier Walk

The dome-shaped building, until recently a branch of Lloyds bank and latterly converted into a restaurant, was originally developed as the Montpellier Spa by Henry Thompson in 1809. Initially it was a simple cottage orné with wooden pillars. This was later replaced with a more elaborate stone building that could be used for balls and assemblies. In 1825 Henry's son, Pearson Thompson, commissioned the celebrated London architect

View from Montpellier Gardens.

J. B. Papworth to add a dome to the building and henceforth it became known as the Rotunda. Measuring 50 feet in diameter, the interior of the dome was partially inspired by the Pantheon in Rome. Today, the concentric pale-blue panels or lacunaria of the dome's interior remain one of the building's most impressive features.

Among the visitors to Thompson's spa was Elizabeth Barrett Browning, who penned the following verse in 1819:

> To taste those lucid streams, for e'en the walk
> To Thompsons wells, a pleasant place to talk.
> Then what bright crowds are seen - when there,
> The young, the old, the plain, the fair –
> 'Neath Esculapius' fostering wings
> All sipping the benignant springs
> And music aids, with her melodious note
> To force the sweet solutions down the throat.

A popular place for concerts before it became a bank, it was probably here that Gustav Holst heard a chamber orchestra for the first time. His father often directed chamber

The interior of the dome, which was partially inspired by the Pantheon.

Satirical sketches by George Cruickshank, 1899.

orchestra concerts here and gave piano recitals at this venue too. Moreover, it was here that the young Holst premiered several of his own compositions, including his 'Duet in D' for two pianos, performed with his father on 13 May 1899.

10. Chapel Arts, Knapp Road

From the seventeenth century, Nonconformity played a significant part in Cheltenham's religious life. Between 1700 and 1900 at least twenty-six Nonconformist chapels existed in the town, of which only six are currently used for worship. Despite this, eleven more of the buildings still survive today, one of which, Chapel Arts, has recently been converted into an arts centre. Formerly known as Bethel Baptist Chapel, the present building, built of brick with a stone front and once featuring a central porchway, was opened in 1820. Today it occupies 1,820 square feet but replaced a smaller chapel less than half this size. The original chapel probably dated from 1701–02 and was run by Tewkesbury Baptist Chapel. In 1753 the Cheltenham Baptists separated from Tewkesbury while still retaining close links with the latter. However, it was only following the construction of the new building and subsequent increase in the town's population that the chapel's congregation started to expand, even forming a breakaway group at Salem Baptist Chapel from 1836. In 1847 the chapel's minister was involved in an act of defiance when he refused on principle to pay church rates, leading to the seizure of some of his goods. It continued to be used as a Baptist chapel until 1951, after which it was used by the Mormons and, in 1965, by the Christadelphians, when it became known as Christadelphian Hall. Today, the building is used for a wide range of art exhibitions and cultural events, with its modern interior design making flexible use of the available space.

Above: One of the town's surviving Nonconformist chapel buildings.

Below: The modernised interior makes flexible use of the available space.

The chapel windows on the west-facing wall.

11. The Beehive, Montpellier Villas

At least 340 licensed premises have traded in Cheltenham at various times between the eighteenth century and the present day. One of the oldest to survive, which also features an interesting façade, is the Beehive. Designed by John Forbes, the architect of Pittville Pump Room, parts of the building reputedly date back to 1822. During the nineteenth century the Beehive acted not only as a venue for other functions including wool auctions that took place in its rear assembly room but also, as was often the case with inns, for occasional hearings of the coroner's court. In 1853, for example, an inquest held there heard the 'melancholy accident' of a lady who died after falling into a well while standing too close to the edge as a workman was repairing a drain. Just over twenty years later the landlord of the Beehive was himself the subject of an inquest after taking his own life while under the influence of drink. In more recent times, perhaps the pub's most famous 'regular' was the poet Cecil Day-Lewis, who taught English at nearby Cheltenham College between 1930 and 1935.

Above: Designed by John Forbes, who also built Pittville Pump Room.

Right: Rear assembly room where wool auctions took place during the nineteenth century.

12. Masonic Hall, Portland Street

Cheltenham's impressive Grade II*-listed Masonic Hall was built between 1820 and 1823 by George Underwood, a Freemason himself, a pupil of John Soane, and also the architect of the town's Holy Trinity Church as well as its Municipal Offices. Outside London, it was the world's first purpose-built Masonic hall, and today has the distinction of being Cheltenham's oldest non-ecclesiastical public building still in use for its original purpose. Its richly decorated interior belies the sombre exterior, which is modelled on a Roman mausoleum and was once described as 'almost intimidating in its eyeless façade'. In fact, the architectural style of the exterior fuses some elements of the Egyptian, characterised by a cant with elevational corners sloping slightly inwards.

As one of the oldest secular fraternities in the world Freemasonry has had a permanent presence in Cheltenham since 1817. Its association with the town was first established following the transfer of one of the foundation lodges dating from 1753 from London and then Abingdon. Meetings originally took place in Sheldon's Hotel on the High Street. The early members played influential roles in the development of the town. Notable local Freemasons have included Dr Edward Jenner, the founder of smallpox vaccination, Dr Henry Boisragon, George IV's physician, and Sir George Dowty, the aeronautical engineer. Four of the town's MPs and two of the principals at Cheltenham College were also Freemasons. Today, there are approximately four hundred members in Cheltenham, affiliated to ten lodges.

The sumptuously decorated interior and furnishings include Cheltenham's oldest organ dating from before 1832. The only recorded non-Masonic use of the building was at the beginning of the twentieth century when it was also hired out as a dance academy.

The windowless front façade, architecturally reflecting the secrecy of the Freemasons.

Detail showing one of the Masonic symbols.

The magnificent sunburst decoration on the high ceiling in the Lodge Room.

13. Thirlestaine House, Bath Road

This fine Grade I-listed building is today owned by Cheltenham College and used both as a venue for concerts, talks and exhibitions, and as accommodation for its art, music and modern languages departments. It was described by the topographical print maker George Rowe in his *Illustrated Cheltenham Guide* (1845) as 'by far the noblest private mansion of which Cheltenham can boast'. Named after the Thirlestane (*sic*) seat of the Scott family, the house was designed by the original owner J. R. Scott, an amateur architect who incorporated copies of carvings from the Parthenon in Athens into its magnificent classical portico. Although construction began in 1823, the building remained unfinished eight years later when Scott died, by which time he had spent nearly £100,000! Despite this, an advertisement at this time claimed that it was the only suitable abode 'worthy of the Repose of His Majesty' if William IV were to honour the town with another royal visit.

In 1838 the house was purchased by Lord Northwick, who enlarged it to house a nationally important collection of 1,500 old master paintings including work by Hogarth, Holbein, Rubens, Titian, Van Dyck and Velásquez. An 1843 guide commented that few private collections in the country could equal 'the number, richness or variety of [its] contents'. The gallery was open to the public when Lord Northwick was not in residence, and generally in the afternoon except on Sundays and 'in very wet or dirty weather' to ensure that the paintings could be seen in favourable light.

Following the death of Lord Northwick in 1859, the entire collection of paintings was sold at an auction that lasted twenty-two days. Eight years later the house was sold to the obsessive collector of books and manuscripts Sir Thomas Phillipps. When his collection was eventually sold, the assets raised £1.6 million. Today, many of the unique manuscripts reside in some of the world's major library collections.

Thirlestaine House, once considered Cheltenham's 'noblest private mansion'.

Above: Advertised in the 1830s as being 'worthy of the Repose of His Majesty'.

Below: Painting by Robert Huskisson showing Lord Northwick's picture gallery, *c.* 1846–47.

14. Cavendish House, Nos 32–48 Promenade

Cavendish House, Cheltenham's oldest department store and now part of the House of Fraser group, first opened as a small shop on the Promenade in 1826 selling 'a choice selection of Silks, Muslins, Shawls, Handkerchiefs, Gauzes, Ribands, Gloves, Lace, Hose and Fancy Articles of English and Foreign Manufacture'.

Originally founded by Thomas Clark and William Debenham, it was the first shop in the Promenade and led the way for the rapid transformation of Cheltenham's most famous thoroughfare from a residential to a commercial street. Although the business initially traded as Clark and Debenham, it was unofficially known from its early days as Cavendish House, the name deriving from the London branch located close to Cavendish Square. The name was officially changed in 1883, and since then the store has been inextricably linked to the town's development as an important and fashionable shopping centre. It has even featured in Helen Ashton's *Return to Cheltenham* (1958) novel where two of the characters 'were measured for new gowns by a black-silken dressmaker in a fitting room lined with looking-glasses'.

During its 190-year-long history, the department store has gradually expanded its premises, the problem of a high water table preventing the possibility of excavating a deep-level basement. At one time, the store boasted the lengthiest shopfront in Cheltenham, which was attractively unified by a balcony with iron railings. However, the premises have also undergone extensive refurbishment programmes at various times, resulting in a mixture of modern bland and even brutalist architecture with only a few surviving elements from the building's Victorian and art nouveau stylings. Finally, as one might expect from such a well-established local firm, Cavendish House has also, over the years, contributed to the town's wider history and development. This has included, for example, providing occasional sponsorship for some of the town's major festivals as well as, during the First World War, contributing a high proportion of its workforce, which numbered forty-two men by March 1915, to enlist in the Army.

View of the Promenade-facing façade, which was refurbished in the 1960s.

Welcome to

CAVENDISH HOUSE
of CHELTENHAM

Right: Promotional card from the 1950s.

Below: Detail from a photograph showing the Victorian frontage.

The Reading and Writing Rooms, Restaurant and every Department of Cavendish House (Cheltenham) is at your Service.

15. Zizzi Restaurant, Suffolk Square

St James's Church, now sympathetically converted into a restaurant, was consecrated in 1830 after its construction was delayed in 1826 owing to a national financial crisis. Built for the developer James Fisher, it initially followed a design by Edward Jenkins, architect of the majority of buildings in Suffolk Square. Its Gothic Revival architecture contrasted with the predominantly neoclassical buildings in the area. One of the technical challenges posed by the building was to construct the roof in a single span across both the nave and aisles. To solve this, Rickman and Hutchinson proposed alterations to Jenkins' original design. However, before Jenkins could complete the project he eloped with the daughter of a wealthy resident, necessitating the work to be completed by another architect – in this

The Gothic Revival church, from a print drawn by George Rowe.

Today, the building has been converted into a restaurant.

case J. B. Papworth, who designed the dome for the Montpellier Rotunda. It was claimed that the church could originally accommodate 1,500 people, the majority of seats being owned by the affluent inhabitants in and around the square. In 1974 the church was closed as a place of worship and became a parish hall after the parish transferred to St Philip and St James's Church. In 2004 it was converted into a restaurant.

16. Pittville Pump Room, East Approach Drive

Pittville Pump Room, often considered Cheltenham's finest Regency building, is reckoned by some to be England's finest spa building. Commissioned in 1825 by the lawyer and wealthy landowner Joseph Pitt as the focal point for his new town of Pittville, it took five years to build at a cost of £90,000. The architect was John Forbes, a local man. Its impressive Ionic columns were based on the Temple of Ilissus. The parapet figures of Hippocrates, 'father' of medicine, Hygeia, goddess of health, and Aesculapius, god of medicine and healing, although post-war copies of the originals, still add to its grandeur. Besides dispensing water for visitors to the spa, in the early days it also provided them with entertainment such as assembly balls, card games and billiards in the pump room, and walks in its pleasure gardens.

Unfortunately, despite its magnificence it could do nothing to halt the decline in fashion for water drinking, which occurred during the 1830s. During the 1840s the Pump Room became part of Joseph Pitt's debt-ridden estate, which was eventually bought from the bank by the borough council in 1889. Thereafter, its future remained uncertain. At one time, its ground-floor ballroom even functioned as a badminton hall. During the Second World War it served as a storage depot for the US Army, the neglect and damage caused during this period almost leading to its demolition. However, restoration work began in 1949 and it was reopened in 1960 by the 7th Duke of Wellington, whose earlier ancestor, the 1st Duke, had witnessed its construction, even speaking with many of the workmen among whom were reportedly veterans of Waterloo.

Today, the Pump Room is one of the town's major venues for concerts and a range of public and private events. The pump that draws water from the 80-feet well was thoroughly overhauled in the 1970s, and the staff endeavour to ensure the waters are still available.

Pittville Pump Room, reckoned by some to be England's finest spa building.

Above left and right: Parapet figures depicting Hippocrates and Aesculapius.

Below: Interior of the dome.

17. St Paul's Church, St Paul's Road

St Paul's Church, whose impressive Ionic columned façade is modelled on the Temple of Ilissus, was designed in 1827 by John Forbes, who had recently designed the Pittville Pump Room. The Grade II*-listed Greek Revival-style building also includes an attractive tower with cupola. The church was built in 1829–31 to cater for one of the poorer quarters of the town, 'where the poor would be certain of welcome', and provided free sittings for

Right: In 1831 the church could accommodate 1,230 people.

Below left: 'The Resurrection' window (detail) by Edward Payne.

Below right: One of the painted panels depicting the Ascension by James Eadie Reid.

the largely artisan congregation in the area. For this reason it was originally known as a 'free' church to distinguish it from other places of worship in the town where most seats were either privately owned or rented, with only a few seats set aside for the poor. When it opened in 1831 it could accommodate 1,230 people, all seated in pews to avoid any distinctions of rank. It is thought to be the last classical-style church to be built in the Gloucester diocese before the Gothic Revival style became the preferred choice for Victorian churches. Thereafter, the classical style was sometimes viewed as 'pagan'.

Interesting features of its interior include an early twentieth-century moveable wrought-iron pulpit set on runners, and a north chapel, formed in 1917, that includes a window of 1963 by the renowned stained-glass artist Edward Payne. Another window of 1906 depicting the Ascension and including flanking painted panels is thought to have been created by the accomplished artist James Eadie Reid.

18. Lansdown Terrace

Lansdown Terrace, described as 'the most original terrace in Cheltenham', was built in stages between 1831 and 1848, the southernmost section (Nos 1–10) being completed first, followed by a middle section (Nos 11–22) and then a northward extension (comprising only No. 23), which was never completed. Part of the Lansdown estate, the town's first planned garden suburb, it was originally developed by Pearson Thompson. Although initially designed by J. B. Papworth, the plan for the estate was greatly altered by the architect brothers Robert and Charles Jearrad. The imposing three-storey-high terrace was designed to reflect the social status of its owners. At the terrace's rear, in Lansdown Terrace Lane, many of the brick buildings, once used as coach houses and stables, have today been successfully converted into offices and garages. One of these was used by the aeronautical engineer Sir George Dowty as a workshop, from which the future Dowty Group was to grow. Among famous residents of Lansdown Terrace was the poet Lady Margaret Sackville, who lived at No. 22 from 1936 until her death in 1963.

Left: The arched passageway next to the house where Margaret Sackville once lived.

Below: Perhaps 'the most original terrace in Cheltenham'.

19. Ashley Manor, No. 252 London Road

Originally dating from 1832 and further extended in 1837–38, this grand villa, which today provides offices and the headmaster's residence for St Edward's Preparatory School, sits in 45 acres of fine parkland opposite the London Inn, which itself dates from the 1830s. The house was probably built by Charles Baker, a surveyor, cartographer and architect from Painswick, for the banker Nathaniel Hartland. The Grade II-listed building was known initially as Oaklands before being renamed Ashley Manor. Its rich, well-preserved interior includes a stone cantilevered staircase, fine stained-glass windows, and an entrance hall with classical-style-decorated saucer domes. In 1958 the house was acquired by the Carmelite order of priests and brothers and converted into Whitefriars School, a Catholic school for boys. In 1987 the school joined forces with the Catholic girls' school at Charlton Park and later became a co-educational preparatory school for St Edward's.

The front façade includes a Perpendicular Gothic-style bay window and oriel.

A detail of The Oaklands from a lithograph by George Rowe.

20. Holst Birthplace Museum, Clarence Road

The terraced house at No. 4 Pittville Terrace (now Clarence Road), currently the only Regency house open to the public in the town, was where the composer Gustav Holst was born on 21 September 1874. He lived there for seven years until the death of his mother in 1882. Originally built in 1832 as part of the Pittville estate, the small Regency house is now a museum run by an independent trust and celebrates his life and work through temporary and permanent displays, which include the piano on which much of *The Planets*, his most celebrated work, was composed. The museum also has a 'Discovery Space' with an interactive kiosk where visitors can access over 3,000 objects in the Holst archive, 'turn the pages' of original Holst manuscripts, and hear recordings of each piece.

The house also depicts the upstairs-downstairs life typical of Victorian and Edwardian households. The living room has been furnished in the style of an 1830s room, before the Holst family moved here, to convey the type of room in which Holst's grandfather, Gustavus Valentine von Holst, would have given harp and piano tuition to Cheltenham's young ladies. His father Adolph von Holst was also well known locally. He taught music at Cheltenham Grammar School, which Holst himself later attended, and the Ladies' College, gave piano recitals at the Assembly Rooms, and was organist at All Saints' Church.

Just before he died, Holst recalled in a letter to Vaughan Williams that it was in his cradle at Pittville Terrace that he first discovered 'that music is a nice thing'. Although not in a central part of town, the house also provided the young Holst with a memorable street scene. Looking out from one of the front windows he noticed a troupe of Morris men with blackened faces dancing outside. It was an incident that gave him a considerable fright and one he was to remember for the rest of his life.

The house was once owned by Holst's mother and family, 1845–95.

Right: Interior of the music room, including the piano Holst used to compose *The Planets*.

Below: The living room furnished in 1830s style.

21. Municipal Offices, Promenade

The magnificent terrace on the west side of the Promenade, considered by some architectural historians to be 'equal to any in Europe', is today largely occupied by the Municipal Offices. Originally called Harward's Buildings, it was named after Samuel Harward, an

Some architectural historians consider this terrace 'equal to any in Europe'.

The Municipal Offices occupy most of the terrace.

Completed in *c.* 1835, Harward's Buildings were named after the developer Samuel Harward.

enterprising businessman who not only established Cheltenham's first circulating library in 1780 but also helped develop both the Promenade and the Sherborne Spa at the beginning of the nineteenth century.

Although it was designed in 1822–23, probably by George Allen Underwood, the sixty-three-bay-long, three-storey high terrace was not completed until around 1835.

Initially, it was used for residential purposes, one town guide claiming that there is 'scarcely another range of houses so architecturally imposing', adding that it was originally designed 'after the fashion of the Louvre'. However, by the beginning of the twentieth century it had become largely commercial and from 1914 onwards the central houses were acquired for conversion into council offices. Nevertheless, the other houses continued to be used for a range of other purposes. As the blue plaque at No. 79 indicates, this included the studio of Hugo van Wadenoyen, a pioneering photographer of Dutch descent who avidly promoted photography as an art form.

Fronted by the attractive formal garden known as the Long Garden, the terrace has occupied centre stage during much of the town's more recent history. It has acted, for example, as the backdrop at memorial events and annual Remembrance Day services as crowds have gathered in the garden to commemorate the dead of the Boer War, the two world wars and more recent conflicts. Additionally, it forms an integral part of the setting for Lady Scott's statue of Edward Wilson, the Cheltenham-born Antarctic explorer who perished with Captain Scott at the South Pole in 1912.

22. Queen's Hotel, Promenade

The Queen's Hotel, which was built in 1837–38 on the site of the Sherborne Spa (later renamed Imperial Spa) at a cost of £47,000, was the biggest hotel in Britain when it was built. Its neoclassical grandeur dominates the view at the southern end of the Promenade.

When built in 1837–38 the Queen's was the biggest hotel in Britain.

Interior showing Pugin wallpaper and Georgian staircase rising above the crowned glass roof.

The current Grade II*-listed building was designed as one of Europe's first purpose-built hotels by the architects Robert and Charles Jearrad. Its impressive façade was modelled on Rome's Temple of Jupiter. Unusually, its pillars and half-columns are elongated across the height of three storeys, but this allowed sufficient space for more than seventy bedrooms and twenty-five sitting rooms. The hotel was named in honour of Queen Victoria whose 1838

The site where the Sebastopol cannons were once sited.

coronation occurred a few weeks before the hotel opened. Indeed, one name considered was the Royal Victoria Hotel. Over the years many distinguished guests have stayed here including Edward VII (when he was Prince of Wales), Prince Louis Jerome Napoleon, Adelina Patti, Sarah Berhardt, Edward Elgar, General Sir Charles Napier, Sir Arthur Conan Doyle and the explorer Fridtjof Nansen.

Perhaps surprisingly given its scale and quality, the hotel initially struggled to make money, and in 1852 it was sold for a paltry £8,400. However, this low price allowed extra investment to be made to restore, alter and improve the building. One of the enhancements made during the mid-nineteenth century was to site a pair of Russian cannons captured at Sebastopol during the Crimean War on plinths in front of the hotel. These were later used as salvaged scrap metal during the Second World War, and today only one of the plinths, now used as a flowerbed, remains.

Although the building has been predominantly used as a hotel, during the First World War it served both as a social refuge for women and a military hospital, while during the Second World War it became an American Services Club once visited by Bob Hope. Today, the building, recently renamed simply Queens, remains one of the town's most important assets, even accommodating the prime minister and a number of cabinet members in 1990.

23. Alma House, Rodney Road

Alma House, one of Cheltenham's most individual buildings, combines elaborate classical Regency architecture with a stunning early twentieth-century interior scheme by Scottish designer George Walton. Built in the mid-1830s as Rodney Villa, it was let

Above: The classical Regency façade belies a stunning early twentieth-century interior scheme.

Below left: Door leading to conservatory (whose exterior is visible from Rodney Road).

Below right: Walton's design draws on the art nouveau and Arts and Crafts movement styles.

to a Miss Richardson, proprietor of a school for 'young ladies'; subsequent occupants included followers of the Revd Francis Close and a series of 'gentry' and other visitors. From the early 1850s to late 1870s retired Vice-Admiral Watts and his family lived in the house. Watts, whose youthful acts of courage featured in several editions of *Deeds of Naval Daring*, renamed the house in celebration of Britain's 1854 Crimean War victory at Alma. The following year, Rodney Road suffered floods, during which, according to the *Cheltenham Chronicle*, 'so impetuous was the rush of waters at the gallant Admiral's house, that the servant who was in the kitchen endeavouring to save her master's property, barely had time to escape with her life'.

In the late 1870s Alma House was acquired by Richard Rogers, a dental surgeon who served five times as Cheltenham's mayor and laid the Town Hall foundation stone. When Rogers retired from dentistry, he transferred his home-cum-surgery to his bachelor nephew George Peake. In the early 1900s Peake put his own stamp on Alma House through commissioning a new 'decorative scheme' from Walton, who was already well known in Glasgow for his work on Miss Cranston's tearooms (including in collaboration with Charles Rennie Mackintosh) and in London for his designs for Eastman-Kodak showrooms. Walton's striking scheme draws on his Glasgow school roots, art nouveau and Arts and Crafts movement (Walton and his brother knew Charles Ashbee of London and Chipping Campden).

The scheme, carried out by Cheltenham firm H. H. Martyn & Co., featured in the prestigious *Studio* magazine 1907 yearbook. Peake, who, as president of Cheltenham Rugby Football Club, was involved with the famous 1905–6 All Blacks British tour, owned Alma House until his death in 1944. Since then, Alma House has been mainly used as offices by a series of tenants and owners, currently a machinery hire company.

24. The Synagogue, Synagogue Lane

Cheltenham's Grade II*-listed synagogue is recognised as 'an outstanding example of a small provincial English synagogue'. Designed by W. H. Knight, also the designer of the town's public library, it opened in 1839 to cater for the growing Jewish population that had been attracted to the town following George III's visit in 1788. Its Ashkenazi furniture, the oldest in the country, dates back to 1761 and some of its plaques are as early as 1727. One of its principal attractions, however, is its dome built by Nicholas Adams, which was described by the *Cheltenham Free Press* as being 'finished in a superior manner with cornice and fretwork'. Although the synagogue closed in 1903 due to a declining congregation, it reopened in 1939 following an influx of refugees and evacuees, and still maintains a flourishing membership today.

Its interior decorations and furnishings include much of historic interest. A decorative curtain dating from the eighteenth century is thought to have been made in India, while English and Hebrew prayer panels contain one for Queen Victoria and the royal family and another from the Yom Kippur service. Another plaque, donated by American servicemen stationed in Cheltenham during the Second World War records the generosity they received from the local community. More recently, an attractive stained-glass window produced in 1957 commemorates the generosity that the Cheltenham Hebrew community received from Joseph Fletcher, a local Gloucester man.

Above: The interior of the magnificent dome, which was built by Nicholas Adams.

Left: Recognised as 'an outstanding example of a small provincial English synagogue'.

Below: One of the Hebrew prayer panels.

25. Faithfull House, Suffolk Square

Occupying almost the entire eastern side of this Regency square, the two sets of Grade II-listed semi-detached residences, which became known as Nos 16–17 and 18–19 Suffolk Mansions in the 1920s and 1930s, are better known today as a Lilian Faithfull residential home. Built in around 1840, probably by the architect Edward Jenkins, they form an integral part of Suffolk Square, one of Cheltenham's most important new estates, which developed in the 1820s at the height of the town's popularity as a spa. The architecturally dominating three-storey buildings overlooking a central green, which since 1923 developed into Ashburne bowling green, convey a sense of exclusivity, space and grandeur.

Suffolk Square was developed by James Fisher, a hotelier who had purchased the Suffolk estate comprising mainly farmland that the Earl of Suffolk had bought from the De la Bere family of Southam in 1808. Coincidentally, one of the Suffolk Mansions that became Faithfull House served as one of the town's leading residential hotels between the 1920s and 1940s. Known as Ware's Hotel after its proprietor William Thomas Ware, the hotel was described as 'the very embodiment of comfort and restful ease' by the *Gloucestershire Echo* when it reopened in 1939 under new ownership, following major refurbishment. At that time, the cream-coloured hotel could accommodate about thirty-five people. It had central heating, eight bathrooms, a lift capable of carrying five people, 1,000 yards of

Below left: The main entrance.

Below right: Embellished handrail, one of the surviving original features.

View of the central green.

undyed Wilton carpet and 'a comprehensive telephone and bell system [that] provide[d] the quickest possible answers to guests' requirements'.

The house's previous use as a hotel made it suitable for conversion into a residential home. By 1957 the four houses had been purchased by the Cheltenham Old Peoples' Housing Society, which had been established by Lilian Faithfull, former principal of Cheltenham Ladies' College and a pioneer in education and social change. Today, the building, renamed Faithfull House in 1951, provides care for approximately seventy residents. Its founder Lilian Faithfull died there in 1952 and is buried in Cheltenham.

26. Railway Station, Queen's Road

Cheltenham's sole remaining railway station, at Lansdown, was built in 1840 to serve the Birmingham & Gloucester (later Midland) Railway, which initially linked Cheltenham to Birmingham and Bristol. It was designed by Samuel Whitfield Daukes and originally included an imposing early Victorian, late Greek Revival Doric portico of nine bays which was unfortunately demolished in 1961. Another station at St James's Square operated between 1847 and 1966 to serve the Great Western Railway. A short line, just over a mile in length, connected the Lansdown and St James's stations, thereby providing Lansdown with an extended link to London. St James's station was the departure point for the *Cheltenham Flyer*, which for a short period during the 1920s achieved the world's fastest timetabled service for the journey between Swindon and London Paddington. Although the Lansdown station has undergone enlargement and refurbishment at various times, it still retains many original features including some fine ironwork. Of particular note are the large bracket supports under the platform bridge, which date back to the original construction in 1840.

Above: The original building included an early Victorian, late Greek Revival Doric portico.

Right: The iron brackets underneath the platform bridge date from 1840.

27. Parabola Arts Centre, Bayshill Road

Originally comprising two semi-detached villas called Bayshill House and Lingwood House, the Cheltenham Ladies' College-owned Parabola Arts Centre is one of the finest buildings in Cheltenham designed in a bold neoclassical style. The villas form part of the

Villa in 'one of the great roads for architecture in all England'.

Detail of the grand colonnaded portico.

Bayshill estate that was constructed between 1834 and the 1850s and contribute to making Bayshill Road what some architectural historians consider to be 'one of the great roads for architecture in all England'. In 2008–09 a £6-million refurbishment and extension project took place by Foster Wilson Architects to transform the villas into a purpose-built performing arts centre, which also provided a learning environment for the college students. Teaching, rehearsing and the theatre's administration today take place in the beautifully restored Grade II*-listed building, while a 325-seat auditorium, which echoes the intimate design of a Georgian theatre, was added as an adjoining extension connected via a glass link building. The shallow recesses in the auditorium's stone façade were designed to reflect the pilasters and cornices of Bayshill House, while the auditorium's limestone-faced outside wall was chosen to complement the stucco of the original house. The building has received several design awards including one from the Royal Institute of British Architects in 2011.

28. Cheltenham College, Bath Road

Cheltenham College was established in 1841, initially occupying three houses in Bayshill Terrace near the town centre. Two years later it moved to its present site on Bath Road following the purchase of land from Lord Northwick, who then owned Thirlestaine House. The college was founded primarily to support progression to university and military or civil service careers in the East India Company. Boys followed either a classical route, with emphasis on the classics, mathematics, history, and Hebrew, or a modern curriculum (also known as military or civil), which comprised subjects such as French, German, drawing, science, Sanskrit and Hindustani.

   The main college building with its imposing central tower was designed in fifteenth-century Gothic style by James Wilson of Bath. Inside, all classes were originally taught in the same single large room known as Big Classical. However, Revd Alfred Barry, the college's first principal and also the son of Sir Charles Barry, the architect of the Houses of Parliament, quickly introduced several improvements including the creation of a separate Juvenile Department to avoid the need for the youngest boys to mix with the older ones. Appropriately, a statue of Barry, who later became a bishop, now adorns the side of the building. By 1868 the college had become so successful that there were 722 students on roll, making it second in size only to Eton. Two years later, the college founded a museum open for public viewing one afternoon a week. This comprised mainly archaeological,

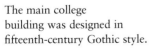
The main college building was designed in fifteenth-century Gothic style.

Above: Initially, the college supported military or East India Company civil service careers.

Left: The statue of Revd Alfred Barry, the college's first principal.

natural history, and geological collections and was an important local resource before the town's public museum was opened.

At the beginning of the Second World War the college buildings were requisitioned by the government and the senior school evacuated to Shrewsbury for two terms. In 1998 it became fully co-educational, a number of girls having been taught at college during the previous thirty years.

29. General Hospital, Sandford Road

Cheltenham's General Hospital was built in Sandford fields in 1848–49 to serve the town's increasing population, which by 1841 had reached 36,000. It replaced Segrave House (now Normandy House) in the Lower High Street and was the last important Classical-style building to be erected in the town. Designed by D. J. Humphris, later the borough surveyor, the building cost £9,000, the funds being raised through voluntary contributions. Shortly after its opening a local guide proudly remarked that this 'hospital is stated by an eminent authority to be not only the cheapest edifice for its purpose, by its economical and useful arrangement of space, but to be a model as respects the correctness of the principles on which it is built'.

Initially, the building was surrounded by 2 acres of gardens but later, part of the grounds was used for keeping chickens and growing fruit and vegetables, which supplied the patients' diet. There were also tennis courts for the staff. However, during the 1920s and 1930s this gave way for building expansion, the extensions to wards and clinics being

The grand portico supported by four fluted Ionic columns.

necessitated by the growth of insurance schemes to cover families' health needs, and the demand for the hospital's services in new fields such as orthopaedics, gynaecology, ophthalmology and cancer services. The art deco-style East Block, for example, which replaced the former Eye, Ear and Throat Hospital, was opened in 1937, blending well with the symmetry of the Classical-style frontage. Originally, the west wing was designated for men and the east wing, which also contained a museum, for women. Among the museum's original collections was Tyson's Pygmie, the skeleton of a young chimpanzee, now on display in London's Natural History Museum. The Bristol-born physician Edward Tyson had analysed this nearly two centuries before the publication of Charles Darwin's *Origin of the Species* (1859), leading him to suggest a link between 'the highest animals' and the 'lowest ranks of men'. Today, just as nearly 170 years ago, the hospital continues to provide vital services to the town.

The building replaced Normandy House (formerly Segrave House) as the town's hospital.

Photograph by Hugo van Wadenoyen, taken during the 1940s.

30. Manor by the Lake, Hatherley Lane

Originally known as Arle Court, the Manor by the Lake was built in 1854–58 in areas of the town now known as The Reddings, Redgrove and Benhall. It was designed by Thomas Penson for the Butt family, who were notable clergymen of the 1800s. Today, the Victorian house and estate serve as a prestigious venue for weddings, business events and social functions. However, during the past 160 years they have been used variously as a private residence, headquarters for Sir George Dowty's aviation empire (now part of Safran) and a breakaway division of Ealing Film Studios.

The original 'Arle Court' name recalls the ancient settlement of Arle, approximately 2 miles to the north-east, long since subsumed within the town. It was there on a site near the present-day Arle Road that an earlier Elizabethan manor house of the same name once stood, part of which has now been incorporated into a house called Arle Court House at No. 23 Kingsmead Road. Although the original Arle Court was demolished in 1881, the link with the Manor by the Lake's past was preserved through the transfer of some of the original Elizabethan fittings to the present building.

During the building's construction, the *Cheltenham Examiner* reported, 'The new Mansion at Arle Court is a splendid specimen of the highly ornamented Elizabethan style and, when finished, it will be one of the largest and most attractive family residences…' Despite this, its Gothic Revival style of architecture annoyed local purists, who disliked the departure from the Regency style. Moreover, they felt that many Victorian architectural rules were being broken, for example through elongating the ground-floor windows and incorporating skylights to make the residence light and airy. Nevertheless, any critics could not fail to be impressed by the high-quality craftmanship of its interior carried out by some of the best woodcarvers and stonemasons in the country. Among these was the local firm of H. H. Martyn, who later produced outstanding work for St Paul's Cathedral and the Houses of Parliament.

'…a splendid specimen of the highly ornamented Elizabethan style'.

Left: Overmantel
(detail) believed to date
from the mid-1600s.

Below: Wooden figures
depicting family
members previously
connected with the
original Arle Court.

31. Montpellier Bandstand, Montpellier Gardens

Built in 1864 to a design by the Ironbridge-based Coalbrookdale Co., Cheltenham's Montpellier Bandstand has the distinction of being the oldest in the country still in regular use, having been rescued from dereliction and restored by Cheltenham Civic Society in 1994. Its attractive features include panels of ornamental ironwork incorporating a design of ladies' heads.

Originally laid out in 1831, Montpellier Gardens were first conceived as an exclusive pleasure ground for visitors to Montpellier Spa, but acquired by Cheltenham Borough Council in 1893. They have always been a place for public entertainment including sports such as tennis, croquet and archery. In fact, the base of the bandstand was used to store archery target bosses for the Cheltenham Archers who practised in the gardens between 1857 and 1934. Later, during the Second World War, it housed a winch that was used to raise or lower one of the town's barrage balloons to the desired altitude. Today, the bandstand still provides a venue for concerts during the summer months.

Britain's oldest bandstand is still in regular use.

Detail of panel showing the design of a lady's head.

32. All Saints' Church, All Saints' Road

All Saints' Church, built from locally quarried Cleeve Hill stone with Bath stone dressings, was consecrated in 1868. A Grade I-listed building in French Gothic style, it is the most spectacular of several buildings in the town designed by the architect John Middleton. Middleton originally intended it to include a 200-feet spire on top of its tower. Although this was never completed, the church's colourful interior, which includes a rose window in the south transept designed by Edward Burne-Jones, as well as other features inspired by the Arts and Crafts movement, provides some breathtaking finishing touches.

All Saints' has a long association with music, which goes back to the church's foundation in 1867 when Adolphus von Holst, Gustav Holst's father, became its organist. A panel inside the church records his appointment. It was also the place where Holst's parents were married on 11 July 1871 and where Gustav was christened on 21 October 1874. The church also played an important part in Gustav's musical development. At the age of

The most spectacular building in Cheltenham designed by John Middleton.

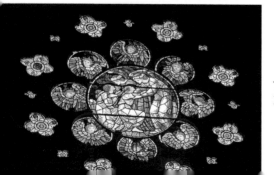

The rose window in the south transept designed by Edward Burne-Jones.

The organ once played by Holst's father.

four, Gustav was brought to All Saints' by his father, who played him a tune that he had previously been taught on his piano at home. Upon hearing it, Gustav shouted out, 'That's my tune!' It was also here where Gustav sang in the church choir, played violin or trombone in the church's small orchestral group and, through his father's position, the place where he practised the organ and tried out his new compositions, including *Four Voluntaries* that he dedicated to his aunt, Nina. Because of this association the Holst Birthplace Museum regularly holds its Holst Birthday Concert here each year on or around 21 September, the composer's birthday.

33. Former County Court, County Court Road

Although the date above the public entrance door to Cheltenham's former county court reads '1870', the building was not completed until the beginning of 1871. The two-storey Grade II-listed building was designed by Thomas Charles Sorby, a London-based architect and the surveyor of county courts, in an austere Italian Renaissance style. It was built on the site of the old Regent Baths, which opened in 1825, allowing patrons to enjoy 'dry sulphur fumigating, medicated vapour and shampooing, salt water, sulphurious, common warm, perpetual cold and warm shower, warm douch, perpetual cold, cold plunging, wooptong or paste, baths …'. When the court opened its doors, the local press considered it to be a vast improvement on its previous building, a 'damp dismal barn' that had been converted from the old baths. Moreover, it was felt that the new building was so impressive that it might well 'have adorned the best street of the town'.

Above: One of the best-preserved examples of a mid-nineteenth-century county court.

Left: Public entrance door with the date when the building was planned to be completed.

The cast lion finials' design was modelled on British Museum railings.

The national system of county courts was formalised in 1848. They were local civil courts for the recovery of small debts. The building was used as a court until the beginning of the twenty-first century. Although latterly a restaurant, little alteration has occurred and it remains one of the best-preserved examples of the style and layout of county courts of the middle of the nineteenth century. The purpose-built courtroom on the first floor still retains much of its original layout and furnishings. In 1888, when new legislation required an increase in the size of the jury from five to eight, it was decided that, rather than making expensive alterations, it was simpler to swap the positions of the jury and the press.

34. Victoria House, No. 1 Gloucester Road

The exuberant red-brick building of the old gasworks offices, now known as Victoria House, is one of the most striking buildings in that quarter of Cheltenham. Reputedly dating from 1855 to 1875 and apparently built by apprentices from the Mechanics' Training School, it displays an extraordinary combination of Gothic Revival, French and baronial styles. Complete with an impressive clock tower, at first glance the Grade II-listed building might be mistaken for a town hall or public library were it not for the inscription of 'Cheltenham Gas Company' intricately laid in decorative terracotta tiles.

In 1819, Cheltenham was one of the first places in the country to pass an act allowing the installation of gas lighting. The construction of the gasworks between Gloucester Road and the High Street followed four years later. In the early years, the company was

Above: This extraordinary building combines Gothic Revival, French and baronial architectural styles.

Left: Detail of the impressive clock tower.

Attractive terracotta tiles used to display the company's name.

guided by Aaron Manby, the first man to build an iron steamship. Excellent success was achieved, as the *Cheltenham Chronicle* proudly reported: 'Never within our recollection has Cheltenham appeared so gay, so brisk, so animated, as in the present season ... we have to notice the recent introduction of the gas light, the brilliant effects of which give a new and captivating appearance to our town by night, and leave us scarcely a desideratum unsupplied'. Although electricity replaced town gas for lighting purposes during the first half of the twentieth century, widespread use of gas for cooking and heating was still made until North Sea gas became available from the 1960s.

The building was converted into offices around 1995 and is now used by a mixture of freelance, startup and established small businesses.

35. Cheltenham Ladies' College, Bayshill Road

Cheltenham Ladies' College, originally known as Cheltenham College for Young Ladies and the first girls' school to be founded on the proprietary system, was established in 1854 at Cambray House, a site now occupied by flats in Cambray Court. In 1873 it transferred to its current purpose-built accommodation in Bayshill, entailing the obliteration of many sites associated with the original spa, all of which had seen better days, including the Pump Room (renamed the Theatre Royal) visited by George III in 1788. The buildings, designed in an ecclesiastical Gothic style by John Middleton, created a striking contrast to the neighbouring terraces built in neoclassical style. Built between 1872 and 1876 with brick faced in Cotswold stone, they initially provided accommodation for 220 pupils and a house for Dorothea Beale, the college's second and longest-serving principal.

Above: The college's ecclesiastical Gothic-style buildings.

Left: One of the statues of famous women created to inspire the students.

View of college skyline including the 1897 observatory used to teach astronomy.

At the opening Miss Beale described the building as a symbol guiding the college's future. 'As each stone stands here in its appointed place,' she said, 'resting on one stone, supporting others; so are we a little community, a spiritual building; ... each has her appointed place, appointed by the Spiritual Architect'. Significantly, Miss Beale believed passionately that attractive surroundings would lead to happy individuals and a good learning environment. Accordingly, she ensured that the interior decoration was filled with some exceptional art and craftmanship, including superb examples of stained glass, mural painting, sculpture and woodcarving. These were carried out by experts in their field such as James Eadie Read, H. H. Martyn, Heaton, Butler and Bayne, and Ernest Gimson. So exacting was Miss Beale's eye for detail that she ensured that even the most mundane or insignificant of features, such as floor grates, were produced with a strong aesthetic design.

Today, the college is a thriving community of 870 pupils. It continues the innovative and pioneering tradition begun by Dorothea Beale. Over the years the expansion of its estate has reflected its changing priorities, whether the construction of an observatory in 1897 to support astronomy, an important part of the college curriculum since the late 1850s, or a new Health and Fitness Centre that will soon be opened.

36. Former Cheltenham College Swimming Baths, College Baths Road

The location of this striking pale-yellow brick building in College Baths Road reflects its former function. Used today by the East Gloucestershire NHS Trust as a repository for health records, it was originally college and then public swimming baths. Designed in 1879 by the local architect W. H. Knight, it had one large pool measuring 80 feet by 60 feet, which was lined with white glazed tiles, as well as fifty changing cubicles, towel washing and drying rooms, and maintenance rooms. Britain was the first country in Europe since the ancient Romans to encourage the construction of public baths when it passed the Baths and Washhouses Act 1846. Although the country's oldest surviving public baths building in Salford dates from 1856, Cheltenham College Baths is one of approximately one hundred that are listed and is considered to be an excellent example of its type, 'the architectural treatment skilfully related to the functional requirements of the building'.

The pool could be filled with 100,000 gallons of water in just under ten hours by a small direct-action engine and pump, which also helped to increase the temperature of the

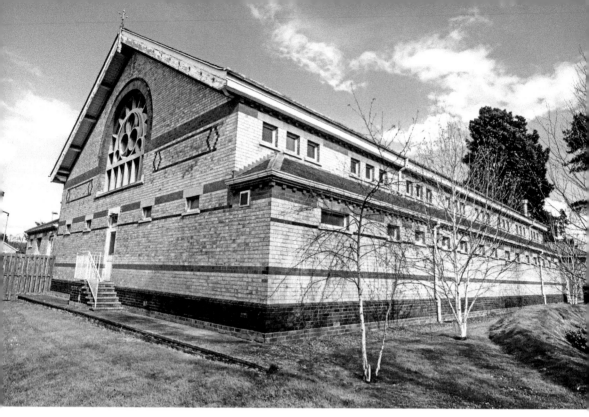

Above: One of the country's oldest surviving public baths building.

Below: Drawing of original building with tall chimney (now dismantled).

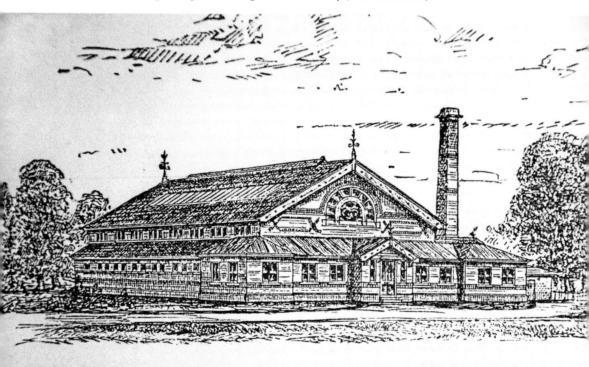

- THE COLLEGE BATHS -
- CHELTENHAM -

Photograph of baths used by Cheltenham College.

water, making it usable for bathing purposes very quickly. The water was supplied from several wells sunk in the sandbed beneath, and was also of drinkable quality. Steam pipes in the interior were used to maintain an air temperature of 15.5°C (60°F), and light and ventilation were provided through windows on the sides, and glass and a cupola in the roof. During the 1990s the college considered various options to convert the baths to other uses such as a boarding house or even a tennis court. In 1998 it was sold to the NHS. Two years later, the adjoining pool keeper's lodge became a charity support centre for cancer patients.

37. Dean Close School, Shelburne Road

Dean Close School was opened in 1886 as a memorial to Francis Close, Cheltenham's well-known evangelical preacher who served as perpetual curate of St Mary's Church (now Cheltenham Minster) for thirty years from 1826 to 1856 and subsequently became Dean of Carlisle. Close was a controversial figure: on the one hand, he preached against Cheltenham's annual horse races and opposed the reconstruction of the town's Theatre Royal after it was destroyed by fire in 1839. On the other, he established many of the town's churches and educational organisations, including Cheltenham College and the College of St Paul and St Mary. Perhaps unsurprisingly, therefore, when a ceremony took place to lay the cornerstone of the new building in 1884 Close's son criticised the town

Above: Main building from Shelburne Road.

Left: Detail from a print by David Gibson.

Portrait of Francis Close (1797–1882) on display at the school.

for its 'lukewarmness' in honouring the name of his father. Nevertheless, upon completion of the building, which was designed by the architect W. H. Knight in a style conceived as 'Elizabethan, effectively but economically treated in red-brick', the local press regaled it as a place 'worthy of the man whose memory it perpetuates … and an honour to the town.' The building itself was said to be 'possessed of sanitary arrangements of almost perfect character', and the headmaster's house, which occupied the right wing, was described as 'substantial and handsome, fitted up with every regard to comfort'.

At its opening the school started with just twelve boys. However, the early success achieved under the school's first headmaster, William Herman Flecker, father of the poet James Elroy Flecker, meant that its student population increased to seventy after the first year and 200 by 1890. Even in its earliest days a broad curriculum was taught including subjects as diverse as scripture, bookkeeping, mathematics, geography, history, French, German, Latin, Greek, natural science, drawing, music, and callisthenics. During the Second World War the building was nearly damaged when five bombs hit the school during air raids. Today there are approximately 900 students and, since 1968, it has been co-educational.

38. Public Library, Clarence Street

Although Cheltenham's first public library was established in 1884 in Liverpool Place in the High Street, it moved to its present site in Clarence Street (then called Manchester Street) following construction in 1887–89 of a new purpose-built building designed by the local architect W. H. Knight. He also designed the local synagogue and college baths, but this building is considered his finest work, demonstrating in particular 'his ability to mix classical with romantic feeling'. A late addition to the design was the inclusion of a tower to enhance the appearance through breaking up the severe line of the roof. Known as the Jubilee Tower having been funded through subscriptions raised for Queen

A building that successfully combines 'classical with romantic feeling'.

The laying of the foundation stone on 21 June 1887.

The statue of William Shakespeare, which was damaged during refurbishment work.

Victoria's Jubilee, a 3-ton block from Cleeve Hill was laid as its foundation stone to mark the celebrations on 21 June 1887.

Since 1855 following the passing of the Public Libraries Act, attempts had been made to gain support for a library that would improve the education of the 'poorer classes'. However, strong objections were made principally on the grounds of cost, especially in the light of potentially higher taxes following the Crimean War as well as a possible negative impact on private libraries, of which the town had several. Furthermore, there were fears that a library for the poor might open on Sundays and even lead to Communism! However, by the beginning of the twentieth century the library had become a valued public amenity with approximately one in ten of the population registered as members of the lending library, and able to access a stock of over 28,000 volumes.

Until 1905 separate Schools of Art and Science were also accommodated on the first floor, the former being positioned to optimise the exposure to northern light before making way for the museum that opened two years later. In 1911, an 8-feet-high statue of William Shakespeare was added to its pediment, although later losing its pen during refurbishment work. Construction of a new central library has been considered recently; instead the current building underwent a major refurbishment in 2008 to create a more modern and brighter interior.

39. Everyman Theatre, Regent Street

The Everyman Theatre, originally styled as the New Theatre and Opera House when it opened in 1891, is the oldest surviving example of the work of Frank Matcham, one of the country's great theatre architects. His two hundred works include London's Palladium and Coliseum. One of the hallmarks of his innovative design was the use of steel cantilevers to support balconies. This enabled increased audience capacity and avoided the spoiling of sightlines through obviating the need for pillars. The building's restrained decoration on its façade contrasts with some glittering splendour in its interior. Particularly noteworthy is the flat ceiling, which, via a clever optical illusion, creates the impression of being dome-shaped.

Cheltenham's long theatrical tradition dates back to the mid-eighteenth century when a converted malthouse and stables close to what is now Pittville Street provided a venue for some of the country's most accomplished actors of the day, including Sarah Siddons and her brother John Kemble. This theatre was renamed the Theatre Royal following

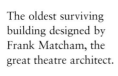

The oldest surviving building designed by Frank Matcham, the great theatre architect.

Left: An example of the building's opulent interior.

Right: The flat ceiling that appears dome-shaped through a clever optical illusion.

George III's visit to Cheltenham in 1788. About a century later, a group of enterprising local citizens were prompted to commission the building of a new theatre after another venue (now occupied by the Princess Hall) was acquired by Cheltenham Ladies' College. The new theatre opened with a performance by Lillie Langtry on 1 October 1891.

During the first half of the twentieth century the theatre prospered, attracting famous actors such as Laurence Olivier and Charlie Chaplin. However, in 1959 the increasing popularity of television threatened its closure. To revive its fortunes, in 1960 it was relaunched as the Everyman following refurbishment and the creation of a new repertory company. Since then the theatre has undergone further restoration and achieved increased success through broadening its range of activities in keeping with the 'Everyman' brand. Today, performances are given in its 700-seat main auditorium or 60-seat Studio Theatre, previously known as The Richardson after the Cheltenham-born actor Ralph Richardson.

40. Strozzi Palace Boutique Suites, No. 55 St George's Place

One of the town's most significant industrial heritage landmarks is this remarkable terracotta brick building, originally modelled on the fifteenth-century Strozzi Palace in Florence, which served as the principal substation to the electricity works at Arle. Cheltenham's first electricity power plant had opened in 1891 near Arle Road. The substation in St George's

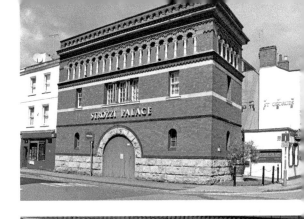

The electricity substation was modelled on the
fifteenth-century Strozzi Palace.

Detail of the decorative pillars.

Side view showing its glass-covered extension.

Place opened in 1895 but twelve years later was converted into offices for the Electricity Company. Since then it was again used as an electricity substation and more latterly, following a recent £750,000 refurbishment, has been converted into luxury hotel suites.

The building was probably designed by the borough engineer Joseph Hall. Following his appointment as chief engineer of Bombay, Hall is also credited with strengthening Cheltenham's close ties with India at the beginning of the twentieth century. He also designed the town's distinctive cast-iron 'dragon and onion' street lamps, good examples of which can be seen nearby in Cheltenham Minster's churchyard.

When the town council held a ceremony to put in place a memorial stone at the Arle central electricity station, the *Cheltenham Chronicle* reported on the potential benefits that the new supply could bring. These included not only the 'clean, cool, and healthy light' but also the possibility of achieving significant cost savings. One example included the possible use of electric light to reduce time spent by clerks on sick leave, estimated at £700 in annual salary savings. Additional cost savings could also accrue from the fact that '[electric] light was free from danger', thereby leading to a considerable reduction in insurance premiums. More significantly, however, electricity compared favourably to gas prices, which included high rental charges for meters. Following the ceremony, the newspaper reported that 'refreshments were served at a buffet, the most remarkable ornament of which was an incandescent light shining in the midst of a large block of ice.' In 1986 a plaque to commemorate its past was unveiled by Revd Wilbert Awdry, author of the Thomas the Tank Engine books.

41. The Brewery, Henrietta Street

Cheltenham's one surviving old brewery building, which today forms the centrepiece of the town's leisure and retail complex known as the Brewery Quarter, was built in 1898 after a devastating fire that originated in the hop room practically destroyed its earlier premises. The brewing of beer in Cheltenham dates back to at least the thirteenth century.

The surviving tower of the 1898 building, now the Brewery Quarter's centrepiece.

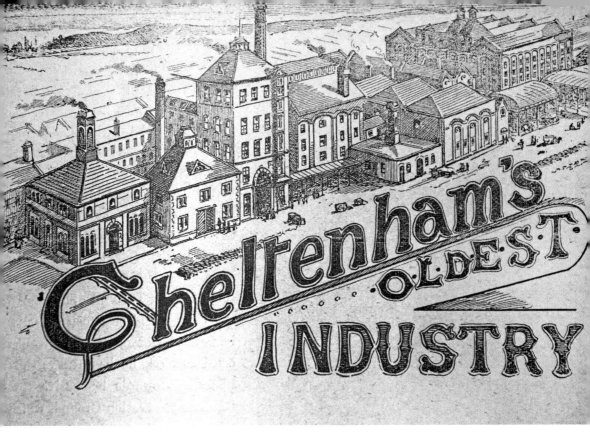

Above: The brewery viewed from above (from an 1897 Cheltenham guide).

Right: The ornate weathervane standing on the ridge of the tower lantern.

From 1760, following the establishment of Gardner's Brewery by the banker John Gardner, the industry was centred in Fleece Lane (now Henrietta Street), where a 35-feet-deep well afforded the daily supply of 27,000 gallons of water. A ledger covering the period between 1767 and 1810 provides a fascinating insight into the host of famous visitors to the brewery. They include the actresses Sarah Siddons and Dorothea Jordan, the statesman Sir Robert Peel, and Dr Edward Jenner, the pioneer of the smallpox vaccine. The Archbishop of Canterbury also patronised the brewery. His bills of £11 8s and £9 3s on 9 and 31 July 1806 respectively were thought by the local press to have arisen because his entourage 'found Cheltenham in the dog-days a thirsty spot, and that the Gardner ale was good stuff as a change from "the waters"'.

From 1888, the firm became a registered company known as the Cheltenham Original Brewery. Following the fire damage on 27 June 1897, estimated at around £50,000, the building was extensively rebuilt using a design by brewery architects Messrs William Bradford & Sons. Concrete jack arching, fireproof floors and wrought-iron roof structures were installed to protect against future disasters. Steam power was also used to drive the pumps, hoists and other moving machinery. The trade prospered greatly, and the company gradually succeeded in absorbing its smaller local rivals. Like many large regional breweries, the Cheltenham Original Brewery proceeded with a number of takeovers well into the post-war years until its own company was acquired by Whitbread in 1963. On 1 October 1998 brewing ceased altogether in Cheltenham, although a number of small local independent breweries have recently begun operating.

42. Town Hall, Imperial Square

Cheltenham's Edwardian baroque Town Hall was built in 1903 as the major venue for the town's cultural life, replacing the Assembly Rooms in the High Street, which were demolished in 1900. The building was designed by Gloucester architect Frederick William Waller and built at a cost of £45,000 by the Cheltenham firm of Collins and Godfrey. The main auditorium, which can accommodate about 900 seated guests, is particularly grand. Its impressive features include a coved ceiling, balconies supported by Corinthian columns, and plaster-cast statues of Edward VII and George V, which were placed in niches on either

One of the major venues for the town's cultural life.

Above: View of the auditorium.

Below: The Doulton ware urns, which originally dispensed different types of mineral water.

side of the stage in 1916. Significantly, the building is also the site of the Central Spa, which was opened in 1906 as part of the Corporation's attempt to revive the spa. To the left of the entrance hall is an octagonal counter with four elaborate Doulton ware urns, only one of which now has a tap (non-functioning) for dispensing the water. Originally, it dispensed different types of mineral water from both Montpellier and Pittville.

As the town's main venue for concerts, lectures and festival events, the Town Hall has often played centre stage to some of Cheltenham's most important historical events. It was here, for example, where Cheltenham's famous Antarctic explorer Dr Edward Wilson gave a memorable lecture in 1906 on the *Discovery* Expedition (1901–04), six years before he perished with Captain Scott at the South Pole. More poignantly, in December 1912 Roald Amundsen gave a lecture about his successful polar conquest two months before the tragic news of the Scott/Wilson expedition reached Cheltenham. It was also here in 1927 where Gustav Holst, another of Cheltenham's famous sons, conducted *The Planets* as part of a festival of his music organised by the local council.

43. The Fire Station, St James's Square

Cheltenham's old fire station, now a restaurant, was built in 1906. It replaced a previous building of around 1840, part of which still survives in the neighbouring building's front façade, which has 'Engine House' carved on it. Throughout the town's history Cheltenham has suffered several major fires. A particularly disastrous one, which came to national attention, occurred in the summer of 1719 in the High Street, and another in 1839 led to

Cheltenham's 1906 fire station cost £500 to build.

Right: The glass atrium now connecting the fire station and engine house.

Below: The fire brigade in front of the newly opened fire station, 1906.

the destruction of the Theatre Royal. Around this time the town commissioners recognised the need for more efficient and reliable fire services, which, until then, had been provided by an insurance company.

The new 1906 building was designed by the office of the borough surveyor (J. S. Pickering) and constructed by the local builders Collins and Godfrey at a cost of £500. The two main entrances were fitted with fourfold glass doors and a similar entrance led to a rear yard used for cleaning the engines. The station officer lived in the older ('Engine House') part of the building. Following its opening the *Gloucestershire Echo* proudly reported that 'very few provincial towns of the size of Cheltenham are now so well equipped with modern fire extinguishing apparatus', adding that 'from the guardroom, on a fire call, the men descend to the ground floor by sliding down a pole, as is usual in all up-to-date stations'.

The station was equipped with three fire engines, the largest of which was a Merryweather 360-gallon steam machine, complete with 300 yards of hose. This was complemented by two smaller hose carts. Additional equipment included stand pipes, jumping sheets, and a 65-feet telescopic fire escape, which was capable of reaching the roofs of the highest residences in the district. The entire workforce consisted of twenty-three men, 'a sturdy set of fellows' divided into two brigades to ensure that one was always ready for duty outside the borough. The station remained operational until 1959 when new headquarters were opened in Keynsham Road.

44. The Wilson, Clarence Street

Cheltenham's first public art gallery was opened in 1899 following the donation of forty-three old master paintings by Baron de Ferrières, a former mayor and MP of the town. He also contributed £1,000 towards the cost of the building. Eight years later, the town's public museum was opened on the first floor of the library building following the transfer of the Schools of Art and Science to new premises in St Margaret's Road. Today, the art gallery and museum is known as The Wilson following a £6.3-million extension in 2012–13. The name was inspired not only by Cheltenham's famous Antarctic explorer Dr Edward Wilson, who perished with Captain Scott at the South Pole in 1912, but also by his father, Dr Edward Thomas Wilson, who campaigned vigorously for the museum and officiated at its opening on 20 June 1907. Wilson was particularly keen to promote a local museum

Front elevation architectural drawing by W. H. Knight, *c.* 1887.

View of the front façade
following its major
refurbishment in 2013.

that had a strong educational purpose. 'Our museum', he said, 'should be no curiosity shop, in which dusty specimens of moth-eaten, ill-stuffed birds and animals, mummy cases, and ancient pickles shock more senses than one'. This vision is continued today through the museum's active learning and outreach programme, its imaginative events, and ever-changing collection displays.

45. The Daffodil, Suffolk Parade

One of Cheltenham's most distinctive and aesthetically pleasing buildings, which has successfully evolved with the changing times, is The Daffodil.

This stylish art deco restaurant is located in the Suffolks. This area initially developed as part of South Town, the original name for one of Cheltenham's artisan districts. Although the present building was completed in 1922, it occupies the site of St James's Lodge, a detached house built before 1841 and later used as a lodging house. By the beginning of the twentieth century Suffolk Parade had become increasingly commercial in character, and in 1922 the house was demolished to make way for the development of the Daffodil

Above: Cheltenham's first purpose-built cinema, now a restaurant.

Below: Photograph showing its original use as a cinema.

The entrance with daffodil floor mosaic.

Picture House, Cheltenham's first purpose-built cinema. Since 1903 films had been shown at various theatres and halls around town, but when the 750-seat cinema opened its doors on 5 October 1922 showing the silent film *Thunderclap*, it became an instant success. Audiences flocked to buy their tickets at a box office adjacent to the street and then entered an attractively tiled lobby that was draped with red velvet curtains. As one cinema-goer recalled during the early 1950s,

> We would sit in the two-and-sixes on the rather grubby seats with a packet of nuts and lose ourselves in fantasy, drama, and romance – generally the showings were of black-and-white British films, made in Pinewood or Ealing – productions of delight and wit and extraordinary characters…

The cinema went from success to success, installing the Western Electric sound system in 1930 at a cost of £5,300 and in 1945 hosting the Cheltenham Film Society, one of the oldest and most successful membership film societies in the country. From the 1950s onwards, however, the emergence of new centrally located cinemas provided increased competition for the Daffodil, and in 1998 it was converted into a restaurant where the proscenium fittings can still be seen.

46. Sandford Lido, Keynsham Road

One of Cheltenham's most loved architectural treasures is the Sandford Park Lido, which continues to serve as one of the oldest and largest outdoor heated swimming pools in the country. Built in 1935 at a cost of £15,700 on land formerly used as allotments, the facilities include three separate pools, the largest measuring 50 metres in length. The unified design of the entire complex, complete with landscaped gardens, sunbathing areas and café, illustrates how outdoor architecture has been used to harness the beneficial effects of air and sunlight.

Although Cheltenham's population only numbered 62,432 at the beginning of the 1930s, the lido managed to attract 100,000 visitors during its first season alone. This was fuelled partly by the increasing popularity of swimming as well as by national and local government campaigns aimed at improving the nation's health and fitness. The word 'lido', which derives from *litus* (Latin meaning 'shore') and evokes the famous Venetian seaside resort, helped to promote a new place where informal relaxation could occur. It also provided a shared space where men, women and children in all sectors of society could come together 'to see and be seen'. Indeed, the concept of public health and inclusion for all is still central to the lido's philosophy today.

Below left: The fountain that originally served to aerate and purify the water.

Below right: A lifeguard dressed in the original 1930s uniform.

The café that opened in 1936 following the lido's successful first season.

During the Second World War the facility provided an important place for recuperation for wounded soldiers and its car park was also used as a petrol depot for passing military convoys. However, during the 1970s the advent of cheap foreign package holidays coupled with severe budgetary pressures affecting local authorities threatened the closure of many lidos throughout the country. To make matters worse, in Cheltenham's case subsequent architectural surveys during the 1980s and 1990s revealed signs of serious structural damage. Fortunately, the lido's future has now been secured – for the medium term at least – thanks to a successful 'Save our Lido' campaign run by a charitable trust formed in 1996. Since then a major refurbishment programme carried out in 2006–07 has helped to restore the lido to its former glory. Ten years later, annual attendance levels have soard to more than 210,000.

47. Eagle Tower, Montpellier Drive

The most conspicuous and controversial of all Cheltenham's buildings is the 161-foot thirteen-storey-high Eagle Tower building, which originally served as the administrative head office and computer centre for Eagle Star Insurance. Opened in 1968 at a cost of £1.7 million as part of the office decentralisation policy of the mid-1960s, it has dominated the town's skyline ever since.

Its construction required the demolition of a hotel and two Regency villas in Montpellier Parade, including *Westal*, the family home of the Antarctic explorer Edward Wilson, who resided there from 1874. However, a much greater proportion of the town's heritage might have been lost had a more radical local council proposal in 1966 to redevelop the town's centre not been successfully opposed.

The angry-looking eagle reflects many of the townspeople's views about this building.

View from Bath Road.

View showing the immense
supporting columns.

Although the building, designed by Stone, Toms & Partners, has been described variously as 'hideous and ill-conceived' and a 'graceless bulk' that is totally out of scale within its immediate vicinity, there is no doubt that the architects achieved part of their aim, which was to signal the dawn of a new era. Furthermore, the exterior concrete work, which so far appears to have avoided serious signs of deterioration, features some interesting decorative detail. Today, the building serves a number of small- and medium-sized businesses.

48. Regent Arcade, High Street

Built between 1982 and 1984 on the site of the historic Plough Hotel and opened in 1985, Cheltenham's 185,000-square foot Regent Arcade is still the town's largest shopping centre. Designed by Roger Dyer Associates, it has over sixty shops, seven restaurants and parking for 500 cars. The present-day building provides an echo of its Regency past through incorporating an approximate facsimile of the Plough's 1825 façade at its main entrance.

Dating from at least 1654, The Plough was Cheltenham's leading hotel and coaching inn, comprising fifty-two bedrooms but just one bathroom. From here, fast stagecoaches such as *The Cheltenham Flyer* set out for London, arriving there within ten and a half

View of the entrance echoing The Plough's Regency-style façade.

hours by 1826. Its extensive yard was reputed to be the largest in the country and could accommodate as many as sixty-two carriages. It was always viewed as the place 'to be seen'. The journalist, C. M. Westmacott, writing under the pseudonym of Bernard Blackmantle in *English Spy* (1826), commented that 'if you wish to make a figure among the Chelts and be thought any thing of, you will, of course, domicile at the Plough'.

Today, the arcade contains several interesting features, including the 45-feet-tall, 3-ton Wishing Fish Clock, which was designed by artist and author Kit Williams, and built by Cheltenham clockmakers Sinclair Harding & Co. Unveiled in 1987, it is reputed to be the world's tallest mechanical clock. The features of the clock include a white duck that lays a never-ending supply of golden eggs, carried down in red egg cups; a family of mice that is constantly trying to evade the attention of a hunting snake; and a huge fish that blows bubbles every half hour to the tune of 'I'm forever blowing bubbles'. Another noteworthy

The Wishing Fish Clock.

item is a small commemorative model of a Gloster E28/39 jet recalling the time in 1940–41 when Frank Whittle designed Britain's first jet engine while he was working in the Regent Motors Garage, another building that predated the shopping centre on this site.

49. GCHQ, Hubble Road

The new Government Communications Headquarters (GCHQ) main building, known as the Doughnut, was completed in 2003 and officially opened by HM the Queen on 24 March 2004. Its architecture has received many accolades, including one describing it as 'a superbly designed and finished building ... perfectly fitting GCHQ's post-Cold War aspiration to be flexible and able to respond to change rapidly, 24 hours a day'. The scale of the building, which houses the largest computer suite outside the USA, is best appreciated from the air. Its roof comprises over 11,000 square metres of aluminium and is based on

Aerial view showing the doughnut shape, aluminium roof and central courtyard.

Right: View of the central 'street' during a family day event.

Below: Illuminated in rainbow colours (marking celebrations against homophobia, transphobia and biphobia).

the design of Wimbledon's Centre Court roof, while its central courtyard is big enough to accommodate the Royal Albert Hall!

GCHQ's first visible association with Cheltenham began in 1950 when staff began transferring from Eastcote under a government relocation scheme. News that it was a Foreign Office department and not a 'less desirable' branch of the civil service was greeted with a sigh of relief by the town's deputy mayor. Initially, GCHQ occupied two sites, at Benhall Farm and Oakley, sites used by the US Army during the war. To accommodate the influx of new residents the council built new housing stock, mostly in the Hester's Way area. Approaching the needs of the twenty-first century, however, a new building was needed, particularly to foster a more collaborative working environment. As one of the three UK Intelligence and Security Agencies, along with MI5 and the Secret Intelligence Service (MI6), GCHQ's success depends on creating innovative solutions to challenging problems. In view of this, a circular design incorporating two concentric rings of open plan offices with a wide 'street' running between them was conceived to facilitate effective knowledge sharing.

GCHQ remains one of the area's largest employers, and its presence encourages other nearby high-tech industries. It also adds a touch of mystery and intrigue to the place, and an international renown that is a far cry from Cheltenham's small market town origins.

50. Princess Royal Stand, Prestbury Park

Prestbury Park, nestled below Cleeve Hill, has been home to Cheltenham's horseraces since 1834, while as far back as 1815 earlier races had taken place on nearby Nottingham Hill. Two hundred years later, as part of a £45-million redevelopment plan for the 'home of jump racing', a new 7,000-capacity five-and-a-half-storey grandstand named in honour of the Princess Royal was opened in November 2015.

General view of the stand during the 2017 Gold Cup Day.

The development, which took nineteen months to complete and involved half a million man hours, was designed for the Jockey Club by Roberts Limbrick Architects. The size and scale of the building may be appreciated from the following statistics: 3,000 spectators can be accommodated at the front of the stand, while the lower-ground floor facilities include 156 toilets.

The new stand is a far cry from 1830 when another impressive grandstand, which was then located on Cleeve Hill where it was visible even from the Promenade, was mysteriously burned down. Although supporters of Francis Close, Cheltenham's evangelical preacher, who spoke out against the 'fatal effects' of attending the races, were suspected, no conclusive proof was ever discovered.

Right: View showing the stand's signage and branding during 2016 Ladies' Day.

Below: The stand taken during day one of The Open, 13 November 2015.

Acknowledgements

I am most grateful to a number of individuals who have commented on drafts, contributed material or made special access arrangements to allow me to visit specific buildings. Particular thanks go to Heather Atkinson, Dr Steven Blake, Oliver Bruce, Fiona Clarke, Sarah Coyle, Sophia Dale, Alex Dimmer, Ann-Rachael Harwood, Laura Herron, Elise Hoadley, Dr James Hodsdon, Georgina Hogg, Martin Hughes, Ian James, Brian McGurk, Rachael Merrison, Eric Miller, Paul Milton, Nick Norman, Christopher Rainey, Rachel Roberts, Anne Strathie, Craig Walker, Shiel Wall, Charles Whitney, Grace Pritchard Woods, and Carol Wright. I am also grateful to the following: Hayley Clemmens for allowing me to take a portrait photograph of her at Sandford Lido (see p. 86); Elizabeth Gillard for permission to quote on p. 85 from *The Tale of a Cheltenham Lady* (Troubador, 2009); and to Pickering & Chatto Publishers for the excerpt of Elizabeth Barrett Browning's poem 'On Thompson's Spas Cheltenham' (1819) reproduced on p. 23.

I am also grateful to the following for copyright permission to use various images: GCHQ Press Office for the Crown Copyright images on pp. 92–93; the Manager, House of Fraser (Cheltenham) for permission to reproduce the historic photograph on p. 33 (bottom); Cheltenham College Archive for permission to reproduce the historic photograph and drawings on p. 31 (top), p. 54 (top), p. 68 (bottom), and p. 69; Sue Ryder Leckhampton Court Hospice for the images on p. 10 and p. 11 (top); Cheltenham Local Studies Centre for permission to reproduce the historic photographs, prints and drawings on p. 15, p. 17 (bottom), p. 21 (middle), p. 34 (top), p. 43, p. 44 (top), p. 56, p. 72 (middle), p. 77 (top), and p. 90 (inset); Martin & Co. for the images on p. 19 (top) and p. 20; Press Association for the images on pp. 94–95; the Headmaster, Dean Close School for permission to reproduce the portrait of Francis Close on p. 71; David Gibson for permission to reproduce a detail of his print on p. 70; Sue Rowbotham for the images on p. 21 (bottom) and p. 81 (bottom); Geoff North for the image on p. 33 (top); The Daffodil for permission to reproduce the historic photograph on p. 84 (bottom); the Headmaster, St Edward's Preparatory School for permission to reproduce the lithograph on p. 39 (bottom); Lloyds Bank for permission to reproduce the satirical sketches on p. 24; and Yale Center for British Art, Paul Mellon Collection for permission to use the image on p. 31 (bottom) showing *Robert Huskisson, Lord Northwick's Picture Gallery at Thirlestaine House*, between 1846 and 1847, oil on canvas.